Memoirs of a Worshipper: 30-Day Devotional

Elder Tyrone Van Buren

Elder Tyrone Van Buren

Memoirs of a Worshipper: 30-Day Devotional

Copyright © 2024 by Tyrone Van Buren

All rights reserved. No part of this book may be reproduced, distributed, or transmitted in any form or by any means, including photocopying, recording, or other electronic or mechanical methods, without the prior written permission of the publisher, except in the case of brief quotations embodied in critical reviews.

ISBN: 9798303478299

FIRST EDITION 2024

Elder Tyrone Van Buren

Memoirs of a Worshipper: 30-Day Devotional

DEDICATION

This book is dedicated to all those who are on a journey to fulfill God's purpose in their lives. To the worshippers who seek to honor God in every moment, and to those who strive to live a life of devotion, gratitude, and love. May this devotional guide you, inspire you, and draw you closer to the heart of God.

Elder Tyrone Van Buren

CONTENTS

	Foreword	i
	Preface	iii
	Acknowledgments	vii
	Introduction	1
Day 1	The Heart of Worship	3
Day 2	A Living Sacrifice	10
Day 3	Worship with Gratitude	17
Day 4	Worship in Spirit and Truth	24
Day 5	The Joy of Worship	31
Day 6	Worship Through Obedience	37
Day 7	Worship in Times of Trouble	44
Day 8	Worship Through Service	51
Day 9	Worship and Community	58
Day 10	Worship Through Prayer	65
Day 11	Worship Through Music	71
Day 12	Worship in Creation	77
Day 13	Worship Through Giving	83
Day 14	Worship in Silence	89

Day 15	Worship and Fasting	95
Day 16	Worship Through Creativity	101
Day 17	Worship and Meditation	107
Day 18	Worship in Fellowship	113
Day 19	Worship and Repentance	120
Day 20	Worship and Sacrifice	126
Day 21	Worship and Trust	132
Day 22	Worship Through Study	138
Day 23	Worship Through Hospitality	144
Day 24	Worship Through Patience	150
Day 25	Worship Through Forgiveness	156
Day 26	Worship Through Gratitude	162
Day 27	Worship Through Hope	168
Day 28	Worship Through Generosity	174
Day 29	Worship Through Compassion	180
Day 30	Worship Through Faith	186
	Biblical Worshippers	193
	Final Thoughts	198

Elder Tyrone Van Buren

FOREWORD

In a world that increasingly pulls us in countless directions, where the noise of daily life can drown out the still, small voice of God, we all need guidance on how to cultivate a deeper, more meaningful relationship with our Creator. When I first encountered Elder Van Buren's words, "Worship is more than a song, a prayer, or a moment in time; it is a lifestyle that encompasses every aspect of our being," I knew this devotional would offer something extraordinary to its readers.

This 30-day devotional is more than just a collection of daily readings—it is a carefully crafted journey that explores the many dimensions of worship, from moments of jubilant praise to seasons of quiet contemplation. I believe it is these necessary seasons of quiet contemplation that we most often overlook. Through personal stories, biblical insights, and practical applications, Elder Van Buren helps us understand that worship is not confined to Sunday mornings or musical expressions but rather encompasses every aspect of our daily lives.

What makes this devotional particularly valuable is its accessibility and depth. Whether you're new to your faith journey or have walked with God for decades, you'll find fresh perspectives and challenging insights that will enrich your understanding of worship. Through these pages you will encounter Immanuel, "God With Us." The author's worshipful heart shines through as he connects ancient biblical truths with contemporary life experiences, making each day's reading both relevant and transformative.

This devotional comes at a crucial time when many are seeking authentic ways to connect with God amidst life's challenges. It serves as both a practical guide and a source of inspiration, encouraging readers to move beyond surface-level religious practices to discover the transformative power of genuine worship.

I believe this book will be a valuable resource for individuals and groups alike, offering fresh insights and practical wisdom for those who desire to deepen their worship experience. May these pages serve as a guide to help you discover the joy, peace, and fulfillment that comes from living a life of authentic worship.

Bishop Henry Ballard Jr.
Family of Churches Fellowship International
Bishop of Christian Education

PREFACE

Welcome to this 30-day journey of worship and reflection. Each day, I will guide you through different aspects of worship, drawing inspiration from scripture, historical context, and personal stories. My goal is to help you deepen your relationship with God and enrich your spiritual life through various forms of worship.

Throughout this journey, you will find:

- **Scripture**: A daily verse to anchor your reflections and guide your worship.

- **Inspiring Insight**: Thought-provoking insights to help you connect with the theme of the day.

- **Historical Context**: Background information to provide a deeper understanding of the scripture and its relevance.

- **Worship Story**: Real-life stories that illustrate the power and impact of worship in different forms.

- **Deeper Thoughts**: Reflections to encourage you to think more deeply about the day's theme and its application in your life.

- **Guided Prayer**: A prayer to help you seek God's presence and guidance in your worship.

- **Practical Exercises**: Action steps, journaling prompts, and discussion questions to help you apply what you've learned and engage with others.

I believe that worship is not just about attending church services or performing religious rituals; it's about living in a way that honors God in every aspect of your life. This journey is designed to help you explore new ways of worshiping God and to experience His presence in your daily life. Each day, you will be encouraged to reflect on your own experiences, engage with scripture, and take practical steps to deepen your worship.

As you embark on this journey, I encourage you to approach each day with an open heart and mind. Allow yourself to be inspired by the stories and insights shared and take the time to engage in the practical exercises. Whether you are new to faith or have been walking with God for many years, I hope this journey will bring you closer to Him and deepen your faith.

Memoirs of a Worshipper: 30-Day Devotional

May each day bring you new insights, deeper connections, and a greater sense of God's presence in your life. I am honored to be a part of your worship journey and look forward to walking with you through these next 30 days of worship and reflection.

- Elder Van Buren

Elder Tyrone Van Buren

ACKNOWLEDGMENTS

I would like to express my deepest gratitude to everyone who has supported and encouraged me throughout the creation of this devotional. To my family and friends, thank you for your unwavering love and belief in my vision. To my church community, your prayers and fellowship have been a constant source of strength and inspiration.

Special thanks to my mentors and spiritual leaders who have guided me on my journey of faith. Your wisdom and counsel have been invaluable. To all the worshippers who have shared their stories and experiences with me, your testimonies have enriched this devotional and made it more meaningful.

Above all, I thank God for His grace, guidance, and the opportunity to serve Him through this work. May this devotional be a blessing to all who read it and draw them closer to His presence.

Elder Tyrone Van Buren

Elder Tyrone Van Buren

INTRODUCTION

Worship is more than a song, a prayer, or a moment in time; it is a lifestyle that encompasses every aspect of our being. It is the way we live, the choices we make, and the love we show to others. "memoirs of a worshipper: a 30-day devotional" is an invitation to embark on a journey of discovering what it means to worship god with your whole heart, mind, and soul.

Throughout this devotional, you will explore various themes of worship, each designed to help you grow in your relationship with god and to see his hand at work in your life. From the joy of worship to the discipline of obedience, from the beauty of creation to the power of community, each day offers a new opportunity to deepen your understanding and practice of worship.

As you engage with the daily readings, reflections, and prayers, i encourage you to take time to meditate on the scriptures, to journal your thoughts, and to seek god's presence in every moment. Let this devotional be a guide to help you cultivate a heart of worship that is genuine, passionate, and transformative.

May your journey through these pages lead you to a deeper, more intimate relationship with god, and may your life be a testament to his glory and grace.

DAY 1: THE HEART OF WORSHIP

Scripture: "God is spirit, and his worshipers must worship in the Spirit and in truth." - John 4:24

Inspiring Insight: True worship isn't confined to songs or rituals; it's about aligning our hearts with God's truth. When Jesus spoke to the Samaritan woman at the well, he emphasized that true worship transcends locations and traditions. It's about a deep, genuine connection with God. Reflect on your daily actions, thoughts, and words. Do they resonate with the truth of who God is? Worship in spirit means engaging with God at a heart level, beyond physical acts, while worship in truth means grounding our lives in the reality of God's word.

Historical Context: In Jesus' time, Jews and Samaritans had significant religious and cultural differences. Samaritans worshipped on Mount Gerizim while Jews worshipped in Jerusalem. By speaking of worship in spirit and truth, Jesus broke down these barriers, emphasizing a more profound, spiritual worship that isn't tied to a specific location but is accessible to all. This conversation with the Samaritan woman was revolutionary, as it challenged the established norms and invited all people to a deeper, more personal relationship with God.

Worship Story: Sarah, a young mother, found herself overwhelmed with the demands of daily life. She realized that her worship had become routine and lacked genuine connection. One day, she decided to take a walk in the park, leaving her phone behind. As she walked, she prayed and reflected on God's goodness. This simple act of worship in spirit and truth transformed her perspective and renewed her relationship with God. Sarah began to incorporate these walks into her daily routine, finding that each step brought her closer to God. Her heart was filled with gratitude and peace, and she discovered that true worship was about connecting with God in the everyday moments of life.

Deeper Thoughts: Reflecting on Sarah's story, we see how stepping away from distractions and intentionally seeking God's presence can transform our worship experience. True worship is about more than just attending church services or singing hymns; it's about cultivating a heart that seeks to honor God in every aspect of our lives. Consider how you can create moments of worship throughout your day, whether it's through prayer, meditation, or simply being mindful of God's presence in your daily activities.

Guided Prayer: Use the following prayer to seek God's presence in your worship: "Heavenly Father, I come before You today with a heart longing to worship You in spirit and in truth. Strip away any pretense or superficiality from my worship. Help me to connect with You deeply, genuinely, and authentically. As I go through my day, may my actions, words, and thoughts reflect a life fully surrendered to You. Teach me to worship You beyond the confines of rituals and traditions, making every moment an offering of love and devotion to You. Let Your truth guide my steps and Your Spirit fill my heart. In Jesus' name, I pray. Amen."

Practical Exercises:

1. **Action Step:** This week, set aside dedicated time each day for personal worship. It could be through singing, praying, or simply sitting in God's presence. Pay attention to how this intentional time of worship affects your relationship with God and your overall sense of peace and joy.
2. **Journaling Prompt:** Reflect on a time when you felt a deep connection with God during worship. What were the circumstances, and how did it impact your relationship with Him? Write down your thoughts and feelings in your journal.
3. **Discussion Question:** How has worship played a role in your spiritual growth? What are some ways you can incorporate worship into your daily routine? Discuss these questions with a friend or small group.

Memoirs of a Worshipper: 30-Day Devotional

NOTES

NOTES

NOTES

DAY 2: A LIVING SACRIFICE

Scripture: "Therefore, I urge you, brothers and sisters, in view of God's mercy, to offer your bodies as a living sacrifice, holy and pleasing to God—this is your true and proper worship." - Romans 12:1

Inspiring Insight: Paul's call to offer our bodies as living sacrifices challenges us to see every action as an act of worship. In ancient times, sacrifices were a way to show devotion and obedience to God. Today, we show our dedication by living in a way that honors Him. This involves our time, resources, and talents, all given back to God in gratitude for His mercy.

Historical Context: The concept of living sacrifices is rooted in the Old Testament, where animal sacrifices were a central part of worship. Paul redefines sacrifice in a spiritual sense, calling believers to a holistic commitment—one that encompasses every aspect of their lives as acts of worship. This shift from physical sacrifices to a life dedicated to God was a radical transformation in the understanding of worship, emphasizing the importance of daily living as an offering to God.

Worship Story: John, a successful businessman, felt a tug on his heart to serve his community. He began volunteering at a local shelter, using his skills to help others find employment. Through this act of service, John discovered a deeper sense of purpose and fulfillment, realizing that his life was a living sacrifice to God. He started to see his work not just as a job, but as a ministry. Every resume he helped write, every interview he coached, became an act of worship. John's dedication inspired others in his community to get involved, creating a ripple effect of service and worship.

Deeper Thoughts: Reflecting on John's story, we see how offering our lives as living sacrifices can transform our daily activities into acts of worship. True worship is about more than just attending church services or performing religious rituals; it's about living in a way that honors God in every aspect of our lives. Consider how you can offer your time, resources, and talents as a living sacrifice to God, and how this commitment can deepen your relationship with Him.

Guided Prayer: Use the following prayer to seek God's guidance in offering your life as a living sacrifice: "Gracious God, in light of Your incredible mercy, I offer my life as a living sacrifice to You. Help me to surrender every part of myself—my thoughts, actions, and desires—as a holy and pleasing offering. Teach me to honor You in all that I do, and guide me to live out my faith authentically. May my life be a reflection of Your grace and love, a testimony of Your transforming power. Strengthen me to resist the ways of the world and to embrace Your will for my life. In Jesus' name, Amen."

Practical Exercises:

1. **Action Step:** This week, identify one area of your life where you can offer your time, resources, or talents as a living sacrifice to God. It could be through volunteering, helping a neighbor, or dedicating time to prayer and reflection. Notice how this act of worship affects your relationship with God and your sense of purpose.

2. **Journaling Prompt:** Reflect on a time when you felt a deep connection with God through an act of service or sacrifice. What were the circumstances, and how did it impact your relationship with Him? Write down your thoughts and feelings in your journal.

3. **Discussion Question:** What areas of your life can you present as a living sacrifice to God? Discuss these questions with a friend or small group.

Elder Tyrone Van Buren

NOTES

NOTES

Elder Tyrone Van Buren

NOTES

DAY 3: WORSHIP WITH GRATITUDE

Scripture: "Give thanks to the Lord, for he is good; his love endures forever." - 1 Chronicles 16:34

Inspiring Insight: Gratitude transforms our perspective and aligns our hearts with God's goodness. Reflect on the small and big blessings in your life and express your thanks daily. Let gratitude be the foundation of your worship.

Historical Context: In Jewish tradition, gratitude was a key component of worship, often expressed through psalms and songs during temple services. Recognizing God's enduring love and goodness, even in challenging times, was essential to maintaining faith. The practice of giving thanks was deeply embedded in the culture, with numerous festivals and rituals dedicated to expressing gratitude to God for His blessings and provision.

Worship Story: Maria, a teacher, faced many challenges in her classroom. Instead of focusing on the difficulties, she began each day by writing down three things she was grateful for. This practice shifted her mindset and allowed her to see God's hand in every situation, filling her heart with joy and gratitude. Maria's attitude of gratitude became contagious, influencing her students and colleagues. She started a gratitude wall in her classroom where students could post what they were thankful for. This simple act of worship through gratitude transformed the atmosphere in her classroom and brought a sense of peace and joy to everyone involved.

Deeper Thoughts: Reflecting on Maria's story, we see how cultivating a heart of gratitude can transform our perspective and bring us closer to God. True worship is about more than just attending church services or performing religious rituals; it's about living in a way that honors God in every aspect of our lives. Consider how you can practice gratitude daily, even in challenging times, and how this attitude can deepen your relationship with God.

Guided Prayer: Use the following prayer to seek God's presence in your worship: "Loving Father, I am overwhelmed by Your goodness and love. Today, I choose to focus on the blessings You have poured into my life. Thank You for Your unwavering love, Your provision, and Your faithfulness. Even in times of difficulty, help me to maintain a heart of gratitude. Open my eyes to see Your hand at work in every situation and fill my heart with thankfulness that overflows into praise. May my gratitude be a continual offering that pleases You. In Jesus' name, Amen."

Practical Exercises:

1. **Action Step:** This week, start a gratitude journal. Each day, write down three things you are grateful for. Reflect on how this practice affects your mindset and your relationship with God.

2. **Journaling Prompt:** Reflect on a time when you felt a deep sense of gratitude. What were the circumstances, and how did it impact your relationship with God? Write down your thoughts and feelings in your

journal.

3. **Discussion Question:** How can you cultivate a heart of gratitude in challenging times? Discuss these questions with a friend or small group.

Memoirs of a Worshipper: 30-Day Devotional

NOTES

Elder Tyrone Van Buren

NOTES

Memoirs of a Worshipper: 30-Day Devotional

NOTES

DAY 4: WORSHIP IN SPIRIT & TRUTH

Scripture: "The hour is coming, and is now here, when the true worshipers will worship the Father in spirit and truth." - John 4:23

Inspiring Insight: Jesus calls us to worship authentically, from our innermost being, and grounded in God's truth. This means our worship should be genuine and reflect the reality of who God is. It's not about the location or outward expressions, but the sincerity of our hearts and minds.

Historical Context: The Jews and Samaritans had deep-rooted animosities, partly due to differences in worship practices. By saying true worshipers will worship the Father in spirit and truth, Jesus pointed to a new era where geographical and ritualistic divides are obsolete, emphasizing a personal, heartfelt worship.

Worship Story: David, a worship leader, realized that his focus had shifted to performance rather than genuine worship. He decided to spend more time in personal prayer and study of the Word, seeking to worship God in spirit and truth. This change brought a new depth and authenticity to his worship, both personally and in leading others. David's renewed focus on genuine worship inspired his congregation to seek deeper connections with God. They began to experience a more profound sense of God's presence during their worship services, transforming their community.

Deeper Thoughts: Reflecting on David's story, we see how shifting our focus from performance to genuine worship can transform our relationship with God. True worship is about more than just attending church services or performing religious rituals; it's about living in a way that honors God in every aspect of our lives. Consider how you can ensure that your worship is genuine and truthful, and how this commitment can deepen your relationship with

Him.

Guided Prayer: Use the following prayer to seek God's presence in your worship: "Dear Lord, I desire to be a true worshiper who honors You in spirit and truth. Purify my heart and let my worship come from a place of deep sincerity and commitment to Your truth. Remove any barriers that keep me from fully engaging with You. Fill me with Your Spirit, and let Your truth illuminate my life. As I worship, let it be a genuine expression of my love and devotion to You. May my life reflect the worship You seek—one that is rooted in Your Word and led by Your Spirit. In Jesus' name, Amen."

Practical Exercises:

1. **Action Step:** This week, dedicate time each day to personal prayer and study of the Word. Focus on worshiping God in spirit and truth, and notice how this practice affects your relationship with Him and your sense of authenticity in worship.

2. **Journaling Prompt:** Reflect on a time when you felt a deep connection with God through genuine worship. What were the circumstances, and how did it impact your

relationship with Him? Write down your thoughts and feelings in your journal.

3. **Discussion Question:** In what ways can you ensure that your worship is genuine and truthful? Discuss these questions with a friend or small group.

Elder Tyrone Van Buren

NOTES

Memoirs of a Worshipper: 30-Day Devotional

NOTES

Elder Tyrone Van Buren

NOTES

DAY 5: THE JOY OF WORSHIP

Scripture: "Shout for joy to the Lord, all the earth. Worship the Lord with gladness; come before him with joyful songs." - Psalm 100:1-2

Inspiring Insight: Worship should be filled with joy and gladness. When we worship God with a joyful heart, we reflect His goodness and love. Think about how you can bring joy into your worship today, whether through singing, dancing, or simply smiling as you pray.

Historical Context: Joyful worship was central to the lives of the Israelites. Festivals, songs, and dances were common expressions of their devotion and thankfulness to God, acknowledging His provision and protection.

Worship Story: Emily, a young girl, loved to dance. She decided to use her talent to worship God, dancing joyfully during her private prayer time. Her joyful expression of worship not only brought her closer to God but also inspired her family and friends to find joy in their own worship practices. Emily's dance became a powerful testimony of the joy that comes from worshiping God with a sincere heart. Her infectious joy spread to her church community, encouraging others to find their own unique ways to express joy in worship.

Deeper Thoughts: Reflecting on Emily's story, we see how expressing joy in worship can transform our relationship with God and inspire others. True worship is about more than just attending church services or performing religious rituals; it's about living in a way that honors God in every aspect of our lives. Consider how you can infuse more joy into your daily worship practices and how this attitude can deepen your relationship with Him.

Guided Prayer: Use the following prayer to seek God's presence in your worship: "Heavenly Father, thank You for the gift of joy that comes from knowing You. Fill my heart with gladness as I worship You today. Let my praise be a reflection of Your greatness and love. May my songs and prayers be filled with the joy that comes from Your presence. Help me to spread this joy to others, showing them the beauty of a life dedicated to worshiping You. In Jesus' name, I pray. Amen."

Practical Exercises:

1. **Action Step:** This week, find a way to express joy in your worship. It could be through singing, dancing, or simply smiling as you pray. Notice how this joyful expression affects your relationship with God and your overall sense of happiness.

2. **Journaling Prompt:** Reflect on a time when you felt a deep sense of joy during worship. What were the circumstances, and how did it impact your relationship with God? Write down your thoughts and feelings in your journal.

3. **Discussion Question:** How can you infuse more joy into your daily worship practices? Discuss these questions with a friend or small group.

Elder Tyrone Van Buren

NOTES

Memoirs of a Worshipper: 30-Day Devotional

NOTES

Elder Tyrone Van Buren

NOTES

DAY 6: WORSHIP THROUGH OBEDIENCE

Scripture: "To obey is better than sacrifice, and to heed is better than the fat of rams." - 1 Samuel 15:22

Inspiring Insight: God values our obedience more than our offerings. True worship is demonstrated through our willingness to follow His commands and live according to His will. Reflect on areas of your life where you can show greater obedience to God.

Historical Context: This scripture is part of Samuel's rebuke of King Saul for disobeying God's instructions. It highlights the principle that God desires our heartfelt obedience over ritualistic offerings, emphasizing a relationship-based worship.

Worship Story: Michael struggled with a decision that required him to choose between a lucrative job offer and a calling to serve in ministry. After much prayer and seeking counsel, he chose to follow God's call to ministry. This act of obedience brought him immense peace and fulfillment, knowing he was honoring God with his life. Michael's story of obedience inspired others in his church to seek God's will in their own lives, leading to a community-wide commitment to living out their faith through obedience.

Deeper Thoughts: Reflecting on Michael's story, we see how choosing obedience over personal gain can transform our relationship with God and inspire others. True worship is about more than just attending church services or performing religious rituals; it's about living in a way that honors God in every aspect of our lives. Consider how you can align your actions more closely with God's commands and how this commitment can deepen your relationship with Him.

Guided Prayer: Use the following prayer to seek God's guidance in offering your life as a living sacrifice: "Lord, I recognize that true worship is shown through my obedience to You. Help me to follow Your commands wholeheartedly. Guide my steps and give me the strength to make choices that honor You. May my life be a testament to my devotion to You. Teach me to listen to Your voice and to obey with a willing heart. Let my actions be a reflection of my love and reverence for You. In Jesus' name, I pray. Amen."

Practical Exercises:

1. **Action Step:** This week, identify one area of your life where you can show greater obedience to God. It could be through making a difficult decision, following a prompting from the Holy Spirit, or committing to a new spiritual discipline. Notice how this act of obedience affects your relationship with God and your sense of peace and fulfillment.

2. **Journaling Prompt:** Reflect on a time when you felt a deep connection with God through an act of obedience. What were the circumstances, and how did it impact your relationship with Him? Write down your thoughts and feelings in your journal.

3. **Discussion Question:** What steps can you

take to align your actions more closely with God's commands? Discuss these questions with a friend or small group.

Memoirs of a Worshipper: 30-Day Devotional

NOTES

Elder Tyrone Van Buren

NOTES

NOTES

DAY 7: WORSHIP IN TIMES OF TROUBLE

Scripture: "Though the fig tree does not bud and there are no grapes on the vines, yet I will rejoice in the Lord, I will be joyful in God my Savior." - Habakkuk 3:17-18

Inspiring Insight: Even in difficult times, we are called to rejoice in the Lord. Worshiping God during hardships demonstrates our trust and faith in His goodness and sovereignty. Reflect on how you can maintain a heart of worship, even when life is challenging.

Historical Context: Habakkuk's prophecy came during a time of impending disaster for Judah. Despite the bleak circumstances, he chose to find joy in God, showcasing a profound trust in God's ultimate plan and goodness. Habakkuk's message reminds us that true worship transcends our current situation and focuses on God's eternal nature and promises.

Worship Story: Jessica, who recently lost her job, was struggling to stay positive. She decided to turn her focus to worship, despite her circumstances. She spent time each day in prayer and praise, thanking God for His faithfulness. This act of worship helped her to trust in God's provision and timing, and she found peace in the midst of her uncertainty. Jessica's story encourages us to find joy in God, even when life's circumstances are bleak. Her commitment to worship in times of trouble drew her closer to God and strengthened her faith.

Deeper Thoughts: Reflecting on Jessica's story, we see how worshiping God during hardships can transform our perspective and bring us closer to Him. True worship is about more than just attending church services or performing religious rituals; it's about living in a way that honors God in every aspect of our lives. Consider how you can practice worship and gratitude during times of trouble, and how this commitment can deepen your relationship with Him.

Guided Prayer: Use the following prayer to seek God's presence in your worship: "God, in the midst of my struggles, help me to find joy in You. Teach me to worship You not only in times of prosperity but also in times of difficulty. Strengthen my faith and remind me of Your unfailing love and sovereignty. Let my worship be an anchor for my soul, grounding me in the truth of Your goodness. May my praises rise above my circumstances, bringing glory to Your name. In Jesus' name, Amen."

Practical Exercises:

1. **Action Step:** This week, dedicate time each day to worship and gratitude, even in the midst of challenges. Focus on praising God for His faithfulness and provision. Notice how this practice affects your relationship with Him and your sense of peace and joy.

2. **Journaling Prompt:** Reflect on a time when you felt a deep connection with God during a difficult period. What were the circumstances, and how did it impact your relationship with Him? Write down your thoughts and feelings in your journal.

3. **Discussion Question:** How can you practice worship and gratitude during times of trouble? Discuss these questions with a friend or small group.

Elder Tyrone Van Buren

NOTES

NOTES

Elder Tyrone Van Buren

NOTES

DAY 8: WORSHIP THROUGH SERVICE

Scripture: "Whatever you do, work at it with all your heart, as working for the Lord, not for human masters." - Colossians 3:23

Inspiring Insight: Serving others is a powerful form of worship. When we serve with a heart of love and dedication, we honor God. Consider how you can serve those around you, whether through small acts of kindness or larger commitments of your time and resources.

Historical Context: In the early church, service was integral to the community. Believers were encouraged to support each other and their neighbors, reflecting God's love through their actions. The apostles often taught about the importance of serving one another, as Jesus demonstrated through His life and ministry.

Worship Story: Michael, a retired engineer, found a new purpose in serving at his local food bank. He used his skills to improve their operations, ensuring that more families received the help they needed. Through his service, Michael felt a renewed sense of joy and fulfillment. He realized that his acts of service were a form of worship, honoring God by helping others. His story reminds us that every act of service, no matter how small, can be a meaningful expression of worship.

Deeper Thoughts: Reflecting on Michael's story, we see how serving others with love and dedication can transform our relationship with God and inspire others. True worship is about more than just attending church services or performing religious rituals; it's about living in a way that honors God in every aspect of our lives. Consider how you can serve others in a way that honors God today, and how this commitment can deepen your relationship with Him.

Guided Prayer: Use the following prayer to seek God's presence in your worship: "Dear Lord, help me to serve others with the same

Memoirs of a Worshipper: 30-Day Devotional

love and dedication that You have shown me. Let my actions reflect Your goodness and grace. Teach me to work wholeheartedly, as if serving You directly. May my service be an act of worship that brings glory to Your name. Inspire me to see every task as an opportunity to honor You and use me to make a difference in the lives of those around me. In Jesus' name, Amen."

Practical Exercises:

1. **Action Step:** This week, find a way to serve others with love and dedication. It could be through volunteering, helping a neighbor, or committing to a new service project. Notice how this act of service affects your relationship with God and your sense of joy and fulfillment.

2. **Journaling Prompt:** Reflect on a time when you felt a deep connection with God through an act of service. What were the circumstances, and how did it impact your relationship with Him? Write down your thoughts and feelings in your journal.

3. **Discussion Question:** How can you serve others in a way that honors God today? Discuss these questions with a friend or

small group.

NOTES

Elder Tyrone Van Buren

NOTES

NOTES

DAY 9: WORSHIP AND COMMUNITY

Scripture: "For where two or three gather in my name, there am I with them." - Matthew 18:20

Inspiring Insight: Worshiping in community strengthens our faith and builds bonds with fellow believers. Gatherings provide support, encouragement, and accountability. Reflect on the importance of community in your worship and consider how you can foster deeper connections.

Historical Context: Early Christians often met in homes for fellowship and worship. These gatherings were crucial for mutual support and growth in faith. The communal aspect of worship helped to strengthen the early church, as believers shared their lives, resources, and faith with one another.

Worship Story: Linda felt isolated in her faith journey until she joined a small group at her church. The fellowship and shared worship experiences transformed her life. She found encouragement and strength in the community, and her faith deepened as a result. Linda's story demonstrates the power of community in worship, reminding us that we are not meant to walk this journey alone.

Deeper Thoughts: Reflecting on Linda's story, we see how engaging with a worship community can transform our faith journey and provide much-needed support and encouragement. True worship is about more than just attending church services or performing religious rituals; it's about living in a way that honors God in every aspect of our lives. Consider how you can engage more actively with your worship community and how this commitment can deepen your relationship with God and others.

Guided Prayer: Use the following prayer to seek God's presence in your worship: "Heavenly Father, thank You for the gift of community. Help me to connect with others in meaningful ways as we gather to worship You. Let our unity be a testament to Your love and grace. Strengthen our bonds and use us to support and encourage one another. May our worship together inspire us to live out our faith boldly and compassionately. In Jesus' name, Amen."

Practical Exercises:

1. **Action Step:** This week, find a way to engage more actively with your worship community. It could be through joining a small group, volunteering for a church event, or simply reaching out to fellow believers for support and encouragement. Notice how this engagement affects your relationship with God and your sense of belonging.

2. **Journaling Prompt:** Reflect on a time when you felt a deep connection with God through community worship. What were the circumstances, and how did it impact your relationship with Him and others? Write down your thoughts and feelings in your journal.

3. **Discussion Question:** How can you

engage more actively with your worship community? Discuss these questions with a friend or small group.

Elder Tyrone Van Buren

NOTES

NOTES

Elder Tyrone Van Buren

NOTES

DAY 10: WORSHIP THROUGH PRAYER

Scripture: "Pray continually, give thanks in all circumstances; for this is God's will for you in Christ Jesus." - 1 Thessalonians 5:17-18

Inspiring Insight: Prayer is a vital component of worship, allowing us to communicate directly with God. It's a practice that should permeate every aspect of our lives. Reflect on how you can make prayer a continuous part of your daily routine.

Historical Context: In Jewish culture, prayer was a daily discipline, often practiced multiple times a day. Early Christians adopted and adapted these practices, emphasizing personal and communal prayer. The apostles encouraged believers to pray continually, seeing it as a lifeline to God.

Worship Story: Samuel, a busy father of three, struggled to find time for prayer. He decided to set aside a few minutes each morning before the household woke up to pray and read the Bible. This quiet time with God became his most cherished part of the day, setting a positive tone for everything that followed. Samuel's story shows how dedicating time to prayer can transform our daily lives and deepen our worship.

Deeper Thoughts: Reflecting on Samuel's story, we see how integrating prayer into our daily routine can transform our relationship with God and bring us closer to Him. True worship is about more than just attending church services or performing religious rituals; it's about living in a way that honors God in every aspect of our lives. Consider how you can integrate prayer more seamlessly into your everyday life and how this commitment can deepen your relationship with Him.

Guided Prayer: Use the following prayer to seek God's presence in your worship: "Lord, help me to cultivate a life of continuous prayer. Teach me to come to You with every need, joy, and concern. Let my prayers be heartfelt and constant, reflecting my dependence on You. Thank You for the privilege of communicating with You and may my prayer life be an act of worship that honors You. Strengthen my resolve to seek Your guidance and express gratitude in all circumstances. In Jesus' name, Amen."

Practical Exercises:

1. **Action Step:** This week, set aside dedicated time each day for prayer. It could be in the morning, during a lunch break, or before bed. Notice how this intentional time of prayer affects your relationship with God and your overall sense of peace and gratitude.

2. **Journaling Prompt:** Reflect on a time when you felt a deep connection with God through prayer. What were the circumstances, and how did it impact your relationship with Him? Write down your thoughts and feelings in your journal.

3. **Discussion Question:** How can you integrate prayer more seamlessly into your everyday life? Discuss these questions with a friend or small group.

NOTES

Memoirs of a Worshipper: 30-Day Devotional

NOTES

Elder Tyrone Van Buren

NOTES

DAY 11: WORSHIP THROUGH MUSIC

Scripture: "Sing to the Lord a new song; sing to the Lord, all the earth." - Psalm 96:1

Inspiring Insight: Music has always been a powerful medium for worship. It allows us to express our deepest emotions and connect with God on a spiritual level. Reflect on how music can be a part of your worship today, whether through singing, playing an instrument, or simply listening to worship songs.

Historical Context: In biblical times, music was an integral part of worship in both the temple and daily life. King David, known for his psalms, exemplified using music to praise God. The Levites, designated as temple musicians, played a crucial role in leading Israel in worship through songs and instruments.

Worship Story: Grace, a talented violinist, used her gift to lead her congregation in worship. She found that music could express what words sometimes could not, bringing people closer to God. Her heartfelt playing not only enhanced the worship experience but also ministered to her own soul, creating a deep, spiritual connection. Grace's story highlights the power of music in worship and encourages us to find our own musical expressions of praise.

Deeper Thoughts: Reflecting on Grace's story, we see how music can transform our worship experience and bring us closer to God. True worship is about more than just attending church services or performing religious rituals; it's about living in a way that honors God in every aspect of our lives. Consider how you can incorporate more music into your daily worship routine and how this commitment can deepen your relationship with Him.

Guided Prayer: Use the following prayer to seek God's presence in your worship: "Heavenly Father, thank You for the gift of music that allows me to express my love and devotion to You. Help me to find new ways to worship You through song. Let the melodies and lyrics draw me closer to You and fill my heart with Your presence. Use music to deepen my worship and inspire me to live a life that glorifies You. In Jesus' name, Amen."

Practical Exercises:

1. **Action Step:** This week, find a way to incorporate more music into your worship. It could be through singing, playing an instrument, or simply listening to worship songs. Notice how this musical expression affects your relationship with God and your overall sense of connection.

2. **Journaling Prompt:** Reflect on a time when you felt a deep connection with God through music. What were the circumstances, and how did it impact your relationship with Him? Write down your thoughts and feelings in your journal.

3. **Discussion Question:** How can you incorporate more music into your daily worship routine? Discuss these questions with a friend or small group.

Elder Tyrone Van Buren

NOTES

NOTES

Elder Tyrone Van Buren

NOTES

DAY 12: WORSHIP IN CREATION

Scripture: "The heavens declare the glory of God; the skies proclaim the work of his hands." - Psalm 19:1

Inspiring Insight: Nature is a powerful testimony to God's creativity and majesty. When we take time to appreciate the beauty of creation, we are reminded of His greatness. Reflect on the ways you can worship God by enjoying and caring for the world He made.

Historical Context: The Psalms often reflect a deep appreciation for nature, seeing it as a direct expression of God's character and power. In ancient Israel, creation was viewed as a testament to God's glory, with elements like the heavens and the earth frequently used in worship and praise.

Worship Story: Tom, an avid hiker, felt closest to God when surrounded by nature. He made a habit of going on weekly hikes, using the time to pray and meditate on God's creation. During one hike, he was struck by the intricate beauty of a simple flower, which led him to praise God for His incredible attention to detail. Tom's story encourages us to find moments in our daily lives to connect with God through His creation.

Deeper Thoughts: Reflecting on Tom's story, we see how appreciating the beauty of creation can transform our worship experience and bring us closer to God. True worship is about more than just attending church services or performing religious rituals; it's about living in a way that honors God in every aspect of our lives. Consider how you can make time to connect with God through nature and how this commitment can deepen your relationship with Him.

Guided Prayer: Use the following prayer to seek God's presence in your worship: "Creator God, thank You for the beauty and wonder of Your creation. Help me to see Your handiwork in the world around me and to worship You through my appreciation and care for nature. Teach me to be a good steward of the earth and to find moments of peace and reflection in Your creation. May the beauty of the world draw me closer to You and remind me of Your greatness. In Jesus' name, Amen."

Practical Exercises:

Action Step: This week, spend time outdoors appreciating God's creation. It could be through a walk in the park, a hike, or simply sitting in your backyard. Notice how this time in nature affects your relationship with God and your overall sense of peace and wonder.

Journaling Prompt: Reflect on a time when you felt a deep connection with God through nature. What were the circumstances, and how did it impact your relationship with Him? Write down your thoughts and feelings in your journal.

Discussion Question: How can you make time to connect with God through nature? Discuss these questions with a friend or small group.

Elder Tyrone Van Buren

NOTES

NOTES

Elder Tyrone Van Buren

NOTES

DAY 13: WORSHIP THROUGH GIVING

Scripture: "Each of you should give what you have decided in your heart to give, not reluctantly or under compulsion, for God loves a cheerful giver." - 2 Corinthians 9:7

Inspiring Insight: Giving is an act of worship that reflects our gratitude and trust in God. When we give cheerfully, we acknowledge His provision and express our love for others. Reflect on how you can practice generosity in your daily life.

Historical Context: In the early church, giving was a crucial way to support the community and those in need. Paul encouraged believers to give generously and joyfully, emphasizing that cheerful giving was a reflection of one's faith and gratitude to God.

Worship Story: Karen, a small business owner, decided to donate a portion of her profits to local charities. She found great joy in supporting causes that aligned with her values and faith. Her generosity not only blessed others but also deepened her own faith and trust in God's provision. Karen's story reminds us that giving can be a joyful and meaningful expression of worship.

Deeper Thoughts: Reflecting on Karen's story, we see how practicing generosity can transform our relationship with God and inspire others. True worship is about more than just attending church services or performing religious rituals; it's about living in a way that honors God in every aspect of our lives. Consider how you can incorporate a spirit of generosity into your worship and how this commitment can deepen your relationship with Him.

Guided Prayer: Use the following prayer to seek God's presence in your worship: "Generous God, thank You for the blessings You have given me. Help me to give cheerfully and generously, as an act of worship and gratitude. Teach me to see opportunities to bless others and to trust in Your provision. May my giving be a reflection of Your love and a testimony to Your faithfulness. In Jesus' name, Amen."

Practical Exercises:

1. **Action Step:** This week, find a way to practice generosity. It could be through donating to a charity, helping a neighbor, or giving your time to a cause you care about. Notice how this act of giving affects your relationship with God and your sense of joy and fulfillment.

2. **Journaling Prompt:** Reflect on a time when you felt a deep connection with God through an act of giving. What were the circumstances, and how did it impact your relationship with Him? Write down your thoughts and feelings in your journal.

3. **Discussion Question:** How can you incorporate a spirit of generosity into your worship? Discuss these questions with a friend or small group.

NOTES

NOTES

Elder Tyrone Van Buren

NOTES

DAY 14: WORSHIP IN SILENCE

Scripture: "Be still, and know that I am God." - Psalm 46:10

Inspiring Insight: Silence is a powerful way to connect with God. In our busy lives, finding moments of stillness allows us to hear His voice and feel His presence. Reflect on how you can incorporate moments of silence into your worship.

Historical Context: Throughout the Bible, moments of silence and solitude were often used by prophets and Jesus Himself to connect deeply with God. These moments allowed them to seek God's guidance and gain clarity in their mission.

Worship Story: Rachel, a corporate executive, found it difficult to quiet her mind amid her hectic schedule. She began setting aside a few minutes each day to sit in silence and meditate on God's word. These moments of stillness became a sanctuary for her soul, bringing her peace and clarity. Rachel's story shows how creating space for silence can deepen our worship and connection with God.

Deeper Thoughts: Reflecting on Rachel's story, we see how creating space for silence can transform our worship experience and bring us closer to God. True worship is about more than just attending church services or performing religious rituals; it's about living in a way that honors God in every aspect of our lives. Consider how you can create more space for silence and stillness in your daily routine and how this commitment can deepen your relationship with Him.

Guided Prayer: Use the following prayer to seek God's presence in your worship: "Loving Father, help me to find moments of silence and stillness in my day. Teach me to be still and know that You are God. In the quiet, let me hear Your voice and feel Your presence. Use these moments to deepen my relationship with

You and to refresh my spirit. May my times of silence be a sacred space where I can worship You with my whole heart. In Jesus' name, Amen."

Practical Exercises:

1. **Action Step:** This week, set aside dedicated time each day for silence and stillness. It could be in the morning, during a lunch break, or before bed. Notice how these moments of quiet affect your relationship with God and your overall sense of peace and clarity.

2. **Journaling Prompt:** Reflect on a time when you felt a deep connection with God through silence and stillness. What were the circumstances, and how did it impact your relationship with Him? Write down your thoughts and feelings in your journal.

3. **Discussion Question:** How can you create more space for silence and stillness in your daily routine? Discuss these questions with a friend or small group.

Elder Tyrone Van Buren

NOTES

NOTES

Elder Tyrone Van Buren

NOTES

DAY 15: WORSHIP AND FASTING

Scripture: "But when you fast, put oil on your head and wash your face, so that it will not be obvious to others that you are fasting, but only to your Father, who is unseen; and your Father, who sees what is done in secret, will reward you." - Matthew 6:17-18

Inspiring Insight: Fasting is a powerful way to draw closer to God, focusing on spiritual growth over physical needs. Reflect on how fasting can enhance your worship and deepen your relationship with God.

Historical Context: Fasting was a common practice in the Bible, used to seek God's guidance, show repentance, and prepare for significant events. Jesus Himself fasted for 40 days before beginning His ministry, setting an example for His followers.

Worship Story: Mark felt a spiritual dryness and decided to embark on a fast to seek God's guidance. During his fast, he spent extra time in prayer and reading scripture. By the end of the fast, Mark felt a renewed sense of purpose and closeness to God. His experience demonstrates how fasting can lead to profound spiritual breakthroughs and a deeper connection with God.

Deeper Thoughts: Reflecting on Mark's story, we see how fasting can transform our worship experience and bring us closer to God. True worship is about more than just attending church services or performing religious rituals; it's about living in a way that honors God in every aspect of our lives. Consider how you can incorporate fasting into your worship routine and how this commitment can deepen your relationship with Him.

Guided Prayer: Use the following prayer to seek God's presence in your worship: "Heavenly Father, teach me the discipline of fasting and its importance in deepening my relationship with You. Help me to focus on You during times of fasting, seeking Your will and drawing closer to Your heart. Let my sacrifice be an act of worship that brings me into greater alignment with Your purposes. Guide me through this spiritual journey and reward my efforts with a deeper understanding of Your love and grace. In Jesus' name, Amen."

Practical Exercises:

1. **Action Step:** This week, consider incorporating a fast into your worship routine. It could be a partial fast, a full fast, or fasting from a specific activity. Use the time you would normally spend on that activity to pray and seek God's guidance. Notice how this practice affects your relationship with Him and your sense of spiritual growth.

2. **Journaling Prompt:** Reflect on a time when you felt a deep connection with God through fasting. What were the circumstances, and how did it impact your relationship with Him? Write down your thoughts and feelings in your journal.

3. **Discussion Question:** How can you incorporate fasting into your worship routine? Discuss these questions with a friend or small group.

Elder Tyrone Van Buren

NOTES

NOTES

NOTES

DAY 16: WORSHIP THROUGH CREATIVITY

Scripture: "In the beginning, God created the heavens and the earth." - Genesis 1:1

Inspiring Insight: Creativity is a divine gift that allows us to express ourselves and reflect God's creativity. Whether through art, writing, or any other creative outlet, use your talents to worship and honor God.

Historical Context: Throughout history, artistic expression has been a significant part of worship, from the intricate designs of the tabernacle to the beautiful hymns and psalms. The creativity demonstrated in the construction of the temple and its adornments reflected the glory and majesty of God.

Worship Story: Alice, an artist, often felt that her work was disconnected from her faith. She decided to start painting scenes from the Bible, using her creativity to meditate on scripture. As she painted, she felt a deeper connection to God and discovered that her art could be a form of worship. Alice's story encourages us to use our creative talents to glorify God and deepen our spiritual lives.

Deeper Thoughts: Reflecting on Alice's story, we see how using our creative talents can transform our worship experience and bring us closer to God. True worship is about more than just attending church services or performing religious rituals; it's about living in a way that honors God in every aspect of our lives. Consider how you can use your creative talents to worship God and how this commitment can deepen your relationship with Him.

Guided Prayer: Use the following prayer to seek God's presence in your worship: "Creator God, thank You for the gift of creativity. Help me to use my talents to bring glory to Your name. Inspire my heart and mind with ideas that reflect Your beauty and majesty. Let my creative expressions be acts of worship that draw me closer to You and inspire others to do the same. May my work honor You and point others to Your greatness. In Jesus' name, Amen."

Practical Exercises:

1. **Action Step:** This week, dedicate time to a creative project that honors God. It could be painting, writing, crafting, or any other creative outlet. Notice how this creative expression affects your relationship with God and your overall sense of fulfillment.

2. **Journaling Prompt:** Reflect on a time when you felt a deep connection with God through a creative activity. What were the circumstances, and how did it impact your relationship with Him? Write down your thoughts and feelings in your journal.

3. **Discussion Question:** How can you use your creative talents to worship God? Discuss these questions with a friend or small group.

NOTES

NOTES

NOTES

DAY 17: WORSHIP AND MEDITATION

Scripture: "I will meditate on your precepts and fix my eyes on your ways." - Psalm 119:15

Inspiring Insight: Meditation on God's word allows us to internalize His teachings and draw closer to Him. Take time each day to meditate on scripture, allowing it to shape your thoughts and actions.

Historical Context: Meditation has been a practice in many religious traditions, including Judaism and Christianity, as a way to deepen one's spiritual life and understanding of God's will. The Psalms are filled with references to meditation on God's laws and precepts, emphasizing its importance in maintaining a close relationship with Him.

Worship Story: Steve, a busy lawyer, found it challenging to balance his hectic schedule with his spiritual life. He began meditating on a verse each day during his lunch break, allowing God's word to bring peace and clarity to his mind. This practice transformed his approach to work and life, grounding him in his faith. Steve's story shows that meditation can be a powerful tool for integrating worship into our daily routines.

Deeper Thoughts: Reflecting on Steve's story, we see how meditation on scripture can transform our worship experience and bring us closer to God. True worship is about more than just attending church services or performing religious rituals; it's about living in a way that honors God in every aspect of our lives. Consider how you can incorporate meditation on scripture into your daily worship routine and how this commitment can deepen your relationship with Him.

Guided Prayer: Use the following prayer to seek God's presence in your worship: "Dear Lord, teach me to meditate on Your word and let it transform my heart and mind. Help me to find stillness and focus as I reflect on Your precepts. Use these moments of meditation to deepen my understanding of Your ways and draw me closer to You. Let Your word be a lamp to my feet and a light to my path. In Jesus' name, Amen."

Practical Exercises:

1. **Action Step:** This week, set aside dedicated time each day for meditation on scripture. It could be in the morning, during a lunch break, or before bed. Notice how this practice affects your relationship with God and your overall sense of peace and clarity.

2. **Journaling Prompt:** Reflect on a time when you felt a deep connection with God through meditation on scripture. What were the circumstances, and how did it impact your relationship with Him? Write down your thoughts and feelings in your journal.

3. **Discussion Question:** How can you incorporate meditation on scripture into your daily worship routine? Discuss these questions with a friend or small group.

Elder Tyrone Van Buren

NOTES

Memoirs of a Worshipper: 30-Day Devotional

NOTES

Elder Tyrone Van Buren

NOTES

DAY 18: WORSHIP IN FELLOWSHIP

Scripture: "And let us consider how we may spur one another on toward love and good deeds, not giving up meeting together, as some are in the habit of doing, but encouraging one another—and all the more as you see the Day approaching." - Hebrews 10:24-25

Inspiring Insight: Fellowship with other believers is a vital aspect of worship. It provides encouragement, accountability, and shared joy. Reflect on how you can strengthen your fellowship with others and worship together.

Historical Context: The early church placed a strong emphasis on fellowship, meeting regularly in homes for prayer, breaking bread, and sharing in each other's lives. These gatherings were essential for the growth and unity of the early Christian communities.

Worship Story: James, who recently moved to a new city, felt disconnected from his faith community. He joined a local church small group and quickly found a sense of belonging and support. Through shared meals, prayers, and worship, James formed deep, meaningful relationships that strengthened his faith. His story reminds us of the importance of fellowship in our worship journey.

Deeper Thoughts: Reflecting on James's story, we see how engaging with a worship community can transform our faith journey and provide much-needed support and encouragement. True worship is about more than just attending church services or performing religious rituals; it's about living in a way that honors God in every aspect of our lives. Consider how you can engage more deeply in fellowship with your faith community and how this commitment can deepen your relationship with God and others.

Guided Prayer: Use the following prayer to seek God's presence in your worship: "Heavenly Father, thank You for the gift of fellowship with other believers. Help me to build strong, supportive relationships within my faith community. Let our time together be filled with encouragement, love, and shared worship. Use our fellowship to spur each other on toward good deeds and deeper faith. May our gatherings be a reflection of Your love and a source of strength for each other. In Jesus' name, Amen."

Practical Exercises:

1. **Action Step:** This week, find a way to engage more deeply in fellowship with your faith community. It could be through joining a small group, volunteering for a church event, or simply reaching out to fellow believers for support and encouragement. Notice how this engagement affects your relationship with God and your sense of belonging.

2. **Journaling Prompt:** Reflect on a time when you felt a deep connection with God through community worship. What were the circumstances, and how did it impact your relationship with Him and others? Write down your thoughts and feelings in your journal.

3. **Discussion Question:** How can you engage more deeply in fellowship with your faith community? Discuss these questions with a friend or small group.

NOTES

Elder Tyrone Van Buren

NOTES

NOTES

DAY 19: WORSHIP AND REPENTANCE

Scripture: "If we confess our sins, he is faithful and just and will forgive us our sins and purify us from all unrighteousness." – 1 John 1:9

Inspiring Insight: Repentance is a crucial part of worship, allowing us to seek God's forgiveness and purification. Reflect on areas of your life that need repentance and bring them before God.

Historical Context: Repentance was a key theme in the teachings of the prophets and Jesus, emphasizing the need for turning away from sin and returning to God. Confession and repentance were integral parts of worship in the early church, fostering spiritual renewal and growth among believers.

Worship Story: David struggled with guilt over past mistakes. He found healing and freedom through repentance, confessing his sins to God and seeking His forgiveness. This act of repentance became a regular part of his worship, drawing him closer to God and allowing him to experience God's grace and mercy. David's story shows the power of repentance in our worship journey.

Deeper Thoughts: Reflecting on David's story, we see how repentance can transform our worship experience and bring us closer to God. True worship is about more than just attending church services or performing religious rituals; it's about living in a way that honors God in every aspect of our lives. Consider what areas of your life require repentance and forgiveness, and how this commitment can deepen your relationship with Him.

Guided Prayer: Use the following prayer to seek God's presence in your worship: "Merciful God, I come before You with a repentant heart. Forgive me for my sins and cleanse me from all unrighteousness. Help me to turn away from my wrongdoings and seek Your path of righteousness. Let my repentance be an act of worship that draws me closer to You. Thank You for Your faithfulness and forgiveness. In Jesus' name, Amen."

Practical Exercises:

1. **Action Step:** This week, take time to reflect on areas of your life that need repentance. Confess your sins to God and seek His forgiveness. Notice how this act of repentance affects your relationship with Him and your sense of peace and renewal.

2. **Journaling Prompt:** Reflect on a time when you felt a deep connection with God through repentance. What were the circumstances, and how did it impact your relationship with Him? Write down your thoughts and feelings in your journal.

3. **Discussion Question:** What areas of your life require repentance and forgiveness? Discuss these questions with a friend or small group.

NOTES

Elder Tyrone Van Buren

NOTES

NOTES

DAY 20: WORSHIP AND SACRIFICE

Scripture: "Greater love has no one than this: to lay down one's life for one's friends." - John 15:13

Inspiring Insight: Sacrifice is a profound act of worship that demonstrates our love and commitment. Reflect on the sacrifices you can make in your life to honor God and serve others.

Historical Context: The concept of sacrifice has deep roots in biblical history, from the sacrifices made in the temple to Jesus' ultimate sacrifice on the cross. The early Christians understood sacrifice as a way to follow Christ's example and to demonstrate their commitment to God's call.

Worship Story: Lisa, a nurse, felt called to volunteer during a health crisis. She sacrificed her time and comfort to serve those in need, often working long hours under challenging conditions. Her selflessness inspired others and demonstrated her deep love for God and humanity. Lisa's story reminds us that true worship often involves sacrifice, and it's in these moments that we reflect Christ's love most clearly.

Deeper Thoughts: Reflecting on Lisa's story, we see how making sacrifices can transform our worship experience and bring us closer to God. True worship is about more than just attending church services or performing religious rituals; it's about living in a way that honors God in every aspect of our lives. Consider what sacrifices you can make to deepen your worship and service to God, and how this commitment can deepen your relationship with Him.

Guided Prayer: Use the following prayer to seek God's presence in your worship: "Lord, help me to understand the true meaning of sacrifice. Teach me to lay down my life for others, just as You laid down Your life for me. Let my sacrifices be acts of worship that bring glory to Your name. Give me the strength and courage to make sacrifices for the sake of love and service. May my life be a reflection of Your sacrificial love. In Jesus' name, Amen."

Practical Exercises:

1. **Action Step:** This week, identify one area of your life where you can make a sacrifice to honor God and serve others. It could be through volunteering, giving up something for the benefit of others, or dedicating time to a cause you care about. Notice how this act of sacrifice affects your relationship with God and your sense of fulfillment.

2. **Journaling Prompt:** Reflect on a time when you felt a deep connection with God through an act of sacrifice. What were the circumstances, and how did it impact your relationship with Him? Write down your thoughts and feelings in your journal.

3. **Discussion Question:** What sacrifices can you make to deepen your worship and service to God? Discuss these questions with a friend or small group.

NOTES

Elder Tyrone Van Buren

NOTES

Memoirs of a Worshipper: 30-Day Devotional

NOTES

DAY 21: WORSHIP AND TRUST

Scripture: "Trust in the Lord with all your heart and lean not on your own understanding." - Proverbs 3:5

Inspiring Insight: Trust is a vital component of worship. It requires us to rely on God's wisdom and plan, even when we don't understand. Reflect on how you can strengthen your trust in God.

Historical Context: Trust in God was a central theme in the lives of biblical figures, from Abraham's journey of faith to the Israelites' reliance on God during their exodus. The wisdom literature, particularly the Proverbs, frequently emphasizes the importance of trusting in God's plan and not relying solely on human understanding.

Worship Story: Rachel, faced with a difficult decision about her career, chose to trust God's guidance over her own understanding. She spent time in prayer and sought wise counsel, ultimately making a choice that felt aligned with God's will. This act of trust deepened her faith and brought her peace. Rachel's story encourages us to lean on God's wisdom and trust His plans for our lives.

Deeper Thoughts: Reflecting on Rachel's story, we see how trusting in God can transform our worship experience and bring us closer to Him. True worship is about more than just attending church services or performing religious rituals; it's about living in a way that honors God in every aspect of our lives. Consider how you can deepen your trust in God in your daily life and how this commitment can strengthen your relationship with Him.

Guided Prayer: Use the following prayer to seek God's presence in your worship: "Heavenly Father, I choose to trust You with all my heart. Help me to lean not on my own understanding but to rely on Your wisdom and guidance. Strengthen my faith and give me the confidence to trust in Your plans, even when they are unclear. Let my trust be an act of worship that honors You and reflects my deep love for You. In Jesus' name, Amen."

Practical Exercises:

1. **Action Step:** This week, identify one area of your life where you can practice trusting God more deeply. It could be a decision you need to make, a challenge you're facing, or a situation that requires patience. Notice how this act of trust affects your relationship with God and your sense of peace.

2. **Journaling Prompt:** Reflect on a time when you felt a deep connection with God through an act of trust. What were the circumstances, and how did it impact your relationship with Him? Write down your thoughts and feelings in your journal.

3. **Discussion Question:** How can you deepen your trust in God in your daily life? Discuss these questions with a friend or small group.

NOTES

NOTES

NOTES

DAY 22: WORSHIP THROUGH STUDY

Scripture: "Do your best to present yourself to God as one approved, a worker who does not need to be ashamed and who correctly handles the word of truth." - 2 Timothy 2:15

Inspiring Insight: Studying God's word is an essential aspect of worship. It helps us to understand His will and apply it to our lives. Reflect on how you can deepen your study of the Bible.

Historical Context: The early church emphasized the importance of studying scripture to grow in faith and understanding. Paul's letters often encouraged believers to be diligent in their study and application of the word. The Bereans were commended for their eagerness to study the scriptures daily to verify the teachings they received.

Worship Story: Sarah, a dedicated student of the Bible, found that her time in study brought her closer to God. She joined a Bible study group where she could discuss and explore scripture in-depth with others. This communal study enriched her understanding and helped her to live out God's word more faithfully. Sarah's story emphasizes the importance of studying scripture as a form of worship.

Deeper Thoughts: Reflecting on Sarah's story, we see how studying scripture can transform our worship experience and bring us closer to God. True worship is about more than just attending church services or performing religious rituals; it's about living in a way that honors God in every aspect of our lives. Consider how you can commit to a deeper study of the Bible as an act of worship and how this commitment can deepen your relationship with Him.

Guided Prayer: Use the following prayer to seek God's presence in your worship: "Lord, inspire me to study Your word diligently. Help me to understand and correctly handle the word of truth. Let my study be an act of worship that draws me closer to You and deepens my faith. Use Your word to guide my life and to transform my heart and mind. May I live out Your teachings with integrity and devotion. In Jesus' name, Amen."

Practical Exercises:

1. **Action Step:** This week, set aside dedicated time each day for studying the Bible. It could be in the morning, during a lunch break, or before bed. Notice how this practice affects your relationship with God and your overall sense of understanding and peace.

2. **Journaling Prompt:** Reflect on a time when you felt a deep connection with God through studying scripture. What were the circumstances, and how did it impact your relationship with Him? Write down your thoughts and feelings in your journal.

3. **Discussion Question:** How can you commit to a deeper study of the Bible as an act of worship? Discuss these questions with a friend or small group.

Memoirs of a Worshipper: 30-Day Devotional

NOTES

Elder Tyrone Van Buren

NOTES

NOTES

DAY 23: WORSHIP THROUGH HOSPITALITY

Scripture: "Do not forget to show hospitality to strangers, for by so doing some people have shown hospitality to angels without knowing it." - Hebrews 13:2

Inspiring Insight: Hospitality is a powerful way to worship God by welcoming and serving others. Reflect on how you can practice hospitality in your daily life.

Historical Context: In biblical times, hospitality was a highly valued practice, essential for survival and community. It was considered a sacred duty to welcome and care for guests. Abraham's hospitality to the three visitors in Genesis 18 is a notable example, where his actions resulted in a divine encounter.

Worship Story: Anna, who lived in a small town, opened her home to travelers and those in need. She hosted meals, provided shelter, and offered a listening ear. Her generous hospitality became known throughout the community as a testament to God's love. Anna's story highlights the impact of opening our hearts and homes to others as a form of worship.

Deeper Thoughts: Reflecting on Anna's story, we see how practicing hospitality can transform our worship experience and bring us closer to God. True worship is about more than just attending church services or performing religious rituals; it's about living in a way that honors God in every aspect of our lives. Consider how you can show hospitality as an act of worship to God and how this commitment can deepen your relationship with Him.

Guided Prayer: Use the following prayer to seek God's presence in your worship: "Heavenly Father, help me to show hospitality to others with a loving and generous heart. Teach me to welcome strangers and to serve those in need, just as You have welcomed and cared for me. Let my hospitality be an act of worship that reflects Your love and grace. Use me to create a welcoming and supportive environment for all who come into my life. In Jesus' name, Amen."

Practical Exercises:

1. **Action Step:** This week, find a way to show hospitality to others. It could be through hosting a meal, offering a helping hand, or simply being a welcoming presence. Notice how this act of hospitality affects your relationship with God and your sense of community.

2. **Journaling Prompt:** Reflect on a time when you felt a deep connection with God through an act of hospitality. What were the circumstances, and how did it impact your relationship with Him? Write down your thoughts and feelings in your journal.

3. **Discussion Question:** How can you show hospitality as an act of worship to God? Discuss these questions with a friend or small group.

NOTES

NOTES

NOTES

DAY 24: WORSHIP THROUGH PATIENCE

Scripture: "Be completely humble and gentle; be patient, bearing with one another in love." - Ephesians 4:2

Inspiring Insight: Patience is a virtue that reflects God's character and love. It allows us to endure challenges and wait on God's timing. Reflect on how you can practice patience as an act of worship.

Historical Context: Patience was a key virtue in biblical teachings, often associated with perseverance in faith and trust in God's promises. The early Christians were encouraged to be patient amidst trials and suffering, knowing that God's timing is perfect and His promises are sure.

Worship Story: Tom, a father of two, often felt frustrated by the demands of parenting. He decided to approach his daily challenges with patience, reminding himself that his children were a gift from God. This shift in mindset transformed his interactions with his family, bringing more peace and love into their home. Tom's story shows that patience can be a powerful act of worship, demonstrating our trust in God's timing and purposes.

Deeper Thoughts: Reflecting on Tom's story, we see how practicing patience can transform our worship experience and bring us closer to God. True worship is about more than just attending church services or performing religious rituals; it's about living in a way that honors God in every aspect of our lives. Consider how you can develop greater patience in your daily life and how this commitment can deepen your relationship with Him.

Guided Prayer: Use the following prayer to seek God's presence in your worship: "Loving Father, help me to be patient in all circumstances. Teach me to bear with others in love and to wait on Your perfect timing. Let my patience be a reflection of Your gentle and enduring love. Strengthen my resolve to persevere through challenges and to trust in Your plans. May my patience be an act of worship that honors You and blesses those around me. In Jesus' name, Amen."

Practical Exercises:

1. **Action Step:** This week, identify one area of your life where you can practice patience. It could be in your interactions with family, at work, or in a challenging situation. Notice how this practice affects your relationship with God and your overall sense of peace and understanding.

2. **Journaling Prompt:** Reflect on a time when you felt a deep connection with God through an act of patience. What were the circumstances, and how did it impact your relationship with Him? Write down your thoughts and feelings in your journal.

3. **Discussion Question:** How can you develop greater patience in your daily life? Discuss these questions with a friend or small group.

Memoirs of a Worshipper: 30-Day Devotional

NOTES

NOTES

NOTES

Day 25: Worship Through Forgiveness

Scripture: "Be kind and compassionate to one another, forgiving each other, just as in Christ God forgave you." – Ephesians 4:32

Inspiring Insight: Forgiveness is a profound act of worship that reflects God's mercy and grace. It allows us to let go of resentment and embrace peace. Reflect on how you can practice forgiveness in your life.

Historical Context: Forgiveness is a central theme in the teachings of Jesus, emphasizing its importance in building relationships and maintaining a healthy community. The parable of the unforgiving servant in Matthew 18:21-35 highlights the necessity of forgiving others as

God has forgiven us.

Worship Story: Linda struggled to forgive a colleague who had wronged her. She decided to pray for the strength to forgive and to release her anger. Over time, she found that forgiveness brought her peace and restored her relationship with her colleague. Linda's story illustrates the healing power of forgiveness and how it can transform our hearts and relationships.

Deeper Thoughts: Reflecting on Linda's story, we see how practicing forgiveness can transform our worship experience and bring us closer to God. True worship is about more than just attending church services or performing religious rituals; it's about living in a way that honors God in every aspect of our lives. Consider how you can practice forgiveness in your relationships as an act of worship and how this commitment can deepen your relationship with Him.

Guided Prayer: Use the following prayer to seek God's presence in your worship: "Merciful Father, teach me to forgive others as You have forgiven me. Help me to release any bitterness and resentment, and to embrace a heart of compassion and kindness. Let my forgiveness be a reflection of Your grace and an act of worship that honors You. Heal my relationships and fill them with Your love and peace. In Jesus' name, Amen."

Practical Exercises:

1. **Action Step:** This week, identify one person you need to forgive and take steps to release any bitterness or resentment. Pray for the strength to forgive and seek reconciliation if possible. Notice how this act of forgiveness affects your relationship with God and your sense of peace.

2. **Journaling Prompt:** Reflect on a time when you felt a deep connection with God through an act of forgiveness. What were the circumstances, and how did it impact your relationship with Him? Write down your thoughts and feelings in your journal.

3. **Discussion Question:** How can you practice forgiveness in your relationships as an act of worship? Discuss these questions with a friend or small group.

Memoirs of a Worshipper: 30-Day Devotional

NOTES

Elder Tyrone Van Buren

NOTES

NOTES

DAY 26: WORSHIP THROUGH GRATITUDE

Scripture: "Give thanks in all circumstances; for this is God's will for you in Christ Jesus." - 1 Thessalonians 5:18

Inspiring Insight: Gratitude transforms our perspective and deepens our worship. It helps us to recognize God's blessings in every situation. Reflect on how you can cultivate a heart of gratitude.

Historical Context: Gratitude was a key component of worship in the early church, often expressed through prayers, songs, and communal gatherings. The Psalms, in particular, are filled with expressions of thanksgiving for God's goodness and faithfulness.

Worship Story: Emily, facing a difficult health diagnosis, chose to focus on gratitude. She kept a gratitude journal and found strength in listing the blessings in her life, big and small. This practice helped her to remain hopeful and positive, even in challenging times. Emily's story demonstrates that gratitude can be a powerful act of worship, bringing us closer to God and transforming our outlook.

Deeper Thoughts: Reflecting on Emily's story, we see how cultivating a heart of gratitude can transform our worship experience and bring us closer to God. True worship is about more than just attending church services or performing religious rituals; it's about living in a way that honors God in every aspect of our lives. Consider how you can maintain an attitude of gratitude in all circumstances and how this commitment can deepen your relationship with Him.

Guided Prayer: Use the following prayer to seek God's presence in your worship: "Gracious God, I thank You for Your countless blessings in my life. Help me to cultivate a heart of gratitude, recognizing Your goodness in every situation. Let my thankfulness be an act of worship that honors You and brings joy to my soul. Teach me to give thanks in all circumstances, trusting in Your perfect plan. In Jesus' name, Amen."

Practical Exercises:

1. **Action Step:** This week, start a gratitude journal. Each day, write down three things you are grateful for. Reflect on how this practice affects your mindset and your relationship with God.

2. **Journaling Prompt:** Reflect on a time when you felt a deep sense of gratitude. What were the circumstances, and how did it impact your relationship with God? Write down your thoughts and feelings in your journal.

3. **Discussion Question:** How can you maintain an attitude of gratitude in all circumstances? Discuss these questions with a friend or small group.

NOTES

NOTES

NOTES

DAY 27: WORSHIP THROUGH HOPE

Scripture: "May the God of hope fill you with all joy and peace as you trust in him, so that you may overflow with hope by the power of the Holy Spirit." - Romans 15:13

Inspiring Insight: Hope is a powerful expression of worship, rooted in our trust in God's promises. It brings joy and peace to our hearts. Reflect on how you can maintain hope in your life.

Historical Context: Hope was a central theme in the letters of Paul, offering encouragement and strength to early Christians facing persecution and trials. The promises of God were a source of hope that helped them endure and remain faithful.

Worship Story: James, who was going through a tough financial season, found hope in God's promises. He clung to verses that spoke of God's provision and faithfulness, and this hope sustained him through difficult times. James's story reminds us that hope is a vital part of our worship, sustaining us and bringing us peace and joy.

Deeper Thoughts: Reflecting on James's story, we see how nurturing hope can transform our worship experience and bring us closer to God. True worship is about more than just attending church services or performing religious rituals; it's about living in a way that honors God in every aspect of our lives. Consider how you can nurture and express hope in your daily worship and how this commitment can deepen your relationship with Him.

Guided Prayer: Use the following prayer to seek God's presence in your worship: "God of hope, fill my heart with joy and peace as I trust in You. Help me to overflow with hope by the power of Your Holy Spirit. Let my hope be a beacon of light in dark times and an act of worship that honors You. Strengthen my faith and keep my eyes fixed on Your promises. May my hope inspire others and draw them closer to You. In Jesus' name, Amen."

Practical Exercises:

Action Step: This week, identify one area of your life where you can nurture hope. It could be through reading and meditating on scriptures that speak of God's promises, praying for strength and guidance, or encouraging others who are going through difficult times. Notice how this practice affects your relationship with God and your overall sense of peace and joy.

Journaling Prompt: Reflect on a time when you felt a deep connection with God through an act of hope. What were the circumstances, and how did it impact your relationship with Him? Write down your thoughts and feelings in your journal.

Discussion Question: How can you nurture and express hope in your daily worship? Discuss these questions with a friend or small group.

NOTES

Elder Tyrone Van Buren

NOTES

NOTES

DAY 28: WORSHIP THROUGH GENEROSITY

Scripture: "You will be enriched in every way so that you can be generous on every occasion, and through us your generosity will result in thanksgiving to God." - 2 Corinthians 9:11

Inspiring Insight: Generosity reflects God's abundant blessings in our lives. It allows us to share His love and provision with others. Reflect on how you can practice generosity as an act of worship.

Historical Context: The early church practiced radical generosity, sharing their resources to support one another and to spread the gospel. Paul often commended and encouraged generous giving as a reflection of God's provision and a means of expressing thanksgiving.

Worship Story: Michael, who had experienced financial success, felt called to give back to his community. He began supporting local ministries and charities, not only with money but also with his time and expertise. His generosity inspired others to give, and he saw firsthand how his acts of worship through giving brought glory to God and helped those in need. Michael's story highlights the impact of generosity and how it can be a powerful expression of worship.

Deeper Thoughts: Reflecting on Michael's story, we see how practicing generosity can transform our worship experience and bring us closer to God. True worship is about more than just attending church services or performing religious rituals; it's about living in a way that honors God in every aspect of our lives. Consider how you can cultivate a spirit of generosity in your daily life and how this commitment can deepen your relationship with Him.

Guided Prayer: Use the following prayer to seek God's presence in your worship: "Generous God, thank You for blessing me abundantly. Help me to be generous on every occasion, sharing Your love and provision with others. Let my generosity be an act of worship that results in thanksgiving to You. Teach me to give freely and joyfully, trusting in Your continued provision. May my generosity reflect Your heart and inspire others to do the same. In Jesus' name, Amen."

Practical Exercises:

1. **Action Step:** This week, find a way to practice generosity. It could be through donating to a charity, helping a neighbor, or giving your time to a cause you care about. Notice how this act of generosity affects your relationship with God and your sense of joy and fulfillment.

2. **Journaling Prompt:** Reflect on a time when you felt a deep connection with God through an act of generosity. What were the circumstances, and how did it impact your relationship with Him? Write down your thoughts and feelings in your journal.

3. **Discussion Question:** How can you cultivate a spirit of generosity in your daily life? Discuss these questions with a friend or small group.

NOTES

Elder Tyrone Van Buren

NOTES

NOTES

DAY 29: WORSHIP THROUGH COMPASSION

Scripture: "Finally, all of you, be like-minded, be sympathetic, love one another, be compassionate and humble." - 1 Peter 3:8

Inspiring Insight: Compassion is a reflection of God's love and kindness. It calls us to care for others with empathy and humility. Reflect on how you can practice compassion in your worship.

Historical Context: Compassion was a defining characteristic of the early Christian community, demonstrated through acts of kindness, charity, and support for the vulnerable. Jesus' ministry was marked by His deep compassion for the marginalized and suffering, setting an example for His followers.

Worship Story: Samantha, a volunteer at a homeless shelter, found deep fulfillment in serving those in need. Her compassion and empathy for the shelter's guests were evident in every interaction. She saw her volunteer work as an extension of her worship, demonstrating God's love to those around her. Samantha's story shows how practicing compassion can be a meaningful act of worship that touches lives and reflects God's heart.

Deeper Thoughts: Reflecting on Samantha's story, we see how practicing compassion can transform our worship experience and bring us closer to God. True worship is about more than just attending church services or performing religious rituals; it's about living in a way that honors God in every aspect of our lives. Consider how you can show compassion as an act of worship in your daily interactions and how this commitment can deepen your relationship with Him.

Guided Prayer: Use the following prayer to seek God's presence in your worship: "Compassionate Father, fill my heart with Your love and kindness. Help me to be sympathetic, loving, and humble in my interactions with others. Let my compassion be an act of worship that reflects Your character and brings comfort to those in need. Teach me to see others through Your eyes and to respond with empathy and care. May my actions bring glory to Your name and draw others to Your love. In Jesus' name, Amen."

Practical Exercises:

1. **Action Step:** This week, find a way to show compassion to others. It could be through volunteering, offering a listening ear, or performing acts of kindness. Notice how this practice affects your relationship with God and your sense of fulfillment.

2. **Journaling Prompt:** Reflect on a time when you felt a deep connection with God through an act of compassion. What were the circumstances, and how did it impact your relationship with Him? Write down your thoughts and feelings in your journal.

3. **Discussion Question:** How can you show compassion as an act of worship in your daily interactions? Discuss these questions with a friend or small group.

Memoirs of a Worshipper: 30-Day Devotional

NOTES

Elder Tyrone Van Buren

NOTES

NOTES

DAY 30: WORSHIP THROUGH FAITH

Scripture: "Now faith is confidence in what we hope for and assurance about what we do not see." - Hebrews 11:1

Inspiring Insight: Faith is the foundation of our worship, giving us confidence in God's promises and assurance in His unseen work. Reflect on how you can strengthen your faith and live it out in your worship.

Historical Context: The "Hall of Faith" in Hebrews 11 recounts the stories of many faithful individuals who trusted in God's promises despite not seeing their fulfillment in their lifetimes. Their unwavering faith serves as an example for believers to remain steadfast in their trust in God.

Worship Story: Alex, who had faced numerous setbacks in his career, chose to stand firm in his faith. He trusted that God had a plan for him, even when the future seemed uncertain. Through prayer and worship, Alex found the strength to persevere, and in time, saw God's hand at work in his life. His story underscores the importance of maintaining faith as an act of worship, trusting in God's promises and timing.

Deeper Thoughts: Reflecting on Alex's story, we see how maintaining faith can transform our worship experience and bring us closer to God. True worship is about more than just attending church services or performing religious rituals; it's about living in a way that honors God in every aspect of our lives. Consider how you can deepen and express your faith as an act of worship and how this commitment can strengthen your relationship with Him.

Guided Prayer: Use the following prayer to seek God's presence in your worship: "Faithful God, help me to grow in my faith and to trust in Your promises with confidence and assurance. Let my faith be the foundation of my worship, guiding my actions and decisions. Teach me to live out my faith boldly, even when I cannot see the outcome. Use my faith to inspire and strengthen those around me. May my life be a testament to Your faithfulness and love. In Jesus' name, Amen."

Practical Exercises:

1. **Action Step:** This week, identify one area of your life where you can practice and strengthen your faith. It could be through trusting God with a decision, stepping out in faith in a new endeavor, or relying on His promises in a challenging situation. Notice how this practice affects your relationship with God and your overall sense of peace and assurance.
2. **Journaling Prompt:** Reflect on a time when you felt a deep connection with God through an act of faith. What were the circumstances, and how did it impact your relationship with Him? Write down your thoughts and feelings in your journal.
3. **Discussion Question:** How can you deepen and express your faith as an act of

worship? Discuss these questions with a friend or small group.

NOTES

# NOTES

NOTES

BIBLICAL WORSHIPPERS

The journey of worship is beautifully illustrated through the lives of biblical figures who demonstrated a true heart of worship in various circumstances. These individuals, despite their flaws and challenges, showed us how to connect with god deeply and authentically. Their stories provide us with powerful examples of how to live a life of worship in our own modern context. By examining their lives, we gain insights into the essence of true worship and how it can shape our relationship with god.

Worship in the bible is portrayed as a multifaceted practice, encompassing praise, prayer, sacrifice, obedience, and acts of service. These biblical figures, through their actions and words, reveal the profound impact that genuine worship can have on our lives.

Worship in the Psalms: David

David, known as a man after god's own heart (1 Samuel 13:14), expressed his worship through psalms and songs. His life, from a shepherd boy to the king of Israel, was characterized by an intimate relationship with god. In psalm 23, David sings of god's guidance and provision, "the lord is my shepherd, i lack nothing." David's psalms (e.g., psalm 51) also reveal his repentance and deep trust in god's mercy, showing us the importance of transparency in our worship.

The Song of Mary: Mary (Mother of Jesus)

Mary's worship is beautifully captured in the Magnificat, where she praises god for his mighty deeds and mercy (Luke 1:46-55). Her song begins, "my soul glorifies the lord and my spirit rejoices in god my savior," reflecting her deep gratitude and submission to god's will. Mary's humble acceptance of god's plan for her life encourages us to respond to god with a heart of worship, trusting in his sovereignty.

The Prayer of Hannah: Hannah

Hannah's story is a profound example of faith and worship through prayer. After years of longing for a child, she prayed fervently and made a vow to dedicate her son to god (1 Samuel 1:10-11). Upon the birth of Samuel, her prayer of thanksgiving (1 Samuel 2:1-10) exalts god's holiness and sovereignty. Hannah's unwavering faith and dedication remind us to turn to god in times of need and to worship him with a grateful heart.

Abraham's Obedience: Abraham

Abraham's worship is exemplified by his obedience to god's commands, even when faced with immense personal sacrifice. In genesis 22, Abraham's willingness to offer his son Isaac as a sacrifice demonstrates his absolute faith and trust in god. When god intervenes, it highlights that worship involves trusting god's plan above our own understanding.

The Leadership of Moses: Moses

Moses led the Israelites in worship and prayer, often interceding on their behalf. In exodus 15, after crossing the red sea, moses leads a song of victory and praise, "i will sing to the lord, for he is highly exalted. Both horse and driver he has hurled into the sea." his leadership in worship teaches us the importance of celebrating god's deliverance and guiding others in worship.

Deborah's Song: Deborah

Deborah, a prophetess and judge, led Israel with wisdom and faith. Her song of victory in judges 5 praises god's power and deliverance, "hear this, you kings! Listen, you rulers! I, even i, will sing to the lord; I will praise the lord, the god of Israel, in song." Deborah's leadership and worship inspire us to praise god boldly and trust in his strength.

Worship in the Prison: Paul and Silas

Paul and Silas exemplified unwavering worship even in dire circumstances. Imprisoned for their faith, they prayed and sang hymns to god, and their worship led to a miraculous release (acts 16:25-26). Their story encourages us to maintain a heart of worship regardless of our situation, trusting that god can work through our praise.

Job's endurance: Job

Despite his immense suffering, job's response was one of worship and trust in god. He declared, "the lord gave and the lord has taken away; may the name of the lord be praised" (job 1:21). Job's steadfast faith in the midst of adversity teaches us to worship god even when life is challenging.

The Devotion of Anna: anna the prophetess

Anna's life of worship is marked by her continual prayer and fasting in the temple. Recognizing Jesus as the messiah, she gave thanks to god and spoke about the child to all who were looking forward to the redemption of Jerusalem (Luke 2:36-38). Anna's devotion encourages us to persist in our worship and to share the good news of Jesus with others.

The Vision of Isaiah: Isaiah

Isaiah's encounter with god in the temple led him to profound worship and a sense of mission. When he saw the lord high and exalted, he responded, "here am i. Send me!" (Isaiah 6:1-8). Isaiah's willingness to serve god demonstrates that worship involves not only praising god but also responding to his call.

FINAL THOUGHTS

Congratulations on completing this 30-day journey of worship and reflection! Your dedication and commitment to deepening your relationship with God through various forms of worship is truly commendable. I hope this journey has been enriching and transformative for you.

As you move forward, remember that worship is not confined to a specific time or place. It is a lifestyle, a continuous expression of your love and devotion to God in every aspect of your life. Whether through music, prayer, acts of kindness, or moments of silence, let your worship be a reflection of your heart's desire to honor and glorify Him.

I pray that you continue to grow in your faith and awareness of your purpose through God. May you find strength and boldness to walk in the path he has set before you, trusting in his guidance and provision. Let your life be a testament to his love and grace, inspiring others to seek and worship him.

As you embark on the next chapter of your spiritual journey, may you experience god's presence in new and profound ways. Thank you for allowing me to be a part of this journey with you. May your worship be ever deepening, your faith ever strengthening, and your heart ever filled with His love.

May God bless you abundantly!

Made in the USA
Columbia, SC
27 January 2025